AF574819

Florida

simply beautiful

Photography by *James Randklev*

ISBN 1-56037-237-0

For more information on our books write: Farcountry Press, P.O. Box 5630, Helena, MT 59604 or call: (800) 654-1105 or visit montanamagazine.com

Created, produced, and designed in the United States. Printed in China.

ABOVE: *The Gulf of Mexico from the Keys.*

TITLE PAGE: *St. George Island State Park.*

FRONT COVER: *Islamorada, Upper Matecumbe Key.*

BACK COVER: *Highlands Hammock State Park.*

Foreword

by James Randklev

When Spanish explorer Ponce de Leon came ashore here in 1513, looking for the elusive "fountain of youth" on the legendary "Isle of Bimini," he named this region *Florida* after Spain's Easter holiday Pascua Florida, which translates "feast of flowers." From the state's northern reaches south to the Keys, brilliant flowers entertain the eyes and nose with their hues and fragrances. Wildflowers adorn open prairies, meadows, and shorelines. Cultivated gardens and homes are no less adorned with brilliant bougainvillea, bird of paradise, and hibiscus, and many botanical gardens enthrall and educate their visitors.

The Everglades, with its river of grass, is one of the largest watersheds in the world. Native Americans named it Pa-hay-Okee, which translates as grassy waters. Along the Tamiami Trail, you can gaze out over the endless expanse of saw grass dotted with hammocks of palms and pines. A warm breeze may grow stronger as huge cumulous clouds form overhead, while this magnificent landscape undulates in rhythmic waves of green. Lake Okeechobee, the main freshwater source for the Everglades, is critical for its survival. Draining the swamps was once thought of as a blessing, but now we realize how critical the entire water cycle is for the birds and fish that flourish here.

Florida's 1,200-mile stretch of coastline—including 2,276 miles of tidal shoreline—far exceeds that of forty-seven other states. Along the Atlantic Coast are broad windswept beaches backed with dunes that sea oats colonize. A string of barrier islands protects many beaches from frequent storms and hurricanes. Canaveral National Seashore on the northern reaches of Merritt Island protects abundant wildlife, including leatherback sea turtles, nesting along its warm sandy beaches. Its Mosquito Lagoon, a shallow salt marsh estuary, hosts deer, raccoons, manatees, egrets, spoonbills, and wintering bald eagles. Amazingly, this natural landscape coexists with the Kennedy Space Center at Merritt Island's southern end.

Florida's Gold Coast represents everything from sun-kissed beaches to opulence in hotels, homes, and recreation. In stark contrast is The Nature Conservancy's property of Blowing Rocks Preserve on Jupiter Island, which protects an unusual outcropping of Anastasia limestone. Miami is an eclectic mix of people, architecture, and history, a melting pot of Cuban, Latin, and European cultures on magnificent beaches and streets.

The Keys' coral islands are laid out like a string of white pearls in a sea that changes from translucent turquoise to deep azure. Islamorada Key, the sport fishing capital of the world, hosts intimate white-sand beaches covered in palms. Big Pine Key is home to the National Key Deer Refuge, where these smallest of all white-tail deer are protected from extinction. Bahia Honda Key, named by the Spanish for its deep bay, appears more like a tropical island in the South Pacific.

Key West is where the Atlantic meets the Gulf of Mexico. This five-by-three-mile island is a Mecca for artists, writers, and anyone else who craves a free-spirited lifestyle. I can think of nowhere else in my travels where celebrating each day's sunset becomes an event. Hundreds of sun worshipers gather along Mallory Docks to watch, sing, and entertain until the last rays of light sink into the cerulean waters. From there, you can go seventy miles across the Gulf by seaplane to explore the Dry Tortugas, a group of tiny islands surrounded by clear waters plied by sharks and sea turtles.

Florida's Gulf Coast is spectacular with its crystal-white beaches stretching from Marco Island and Naples north beyond Sarasota, St. Petersburg, and westward to Panama City and Pensacola in the Panhandle. Coastal Islands like Sanibel offer endless hours of shell collecting and recreation along their quiet shores. For contrast, view European art objects in and around circus king John Ringling's Renaissance-style estate and museum of fine art at Sarasota.

Projecting into Tampa Bay like an inverted pyramid, St. Petersburg's The Pier (as locals call it) is a focal point for shopping, good meals, and sightseeing. Across the bay is Tampa, where the historic district of Ybor City glimmers with detailed ceramic-tile storefronts. Farther up the coast, the sponge fishing village of Tarpon Springs honors its Greek founders with delicious traditional foods.

Sprawled along Apalachee Bay, 90,000-acre St. Marks National Wildlife Refuge is a birding paradise, where 300 species nest or pass by on their migratory routes.

St. George Island State Park draws visitors into an intimate

A great blue heron in Mosquito Lagoon on Canaveral National Seashore.

coastal landscape of gently sloping beaches caressed by golden sea oats dancing in the Gulf breeze. Shell fragments washed ashore lay scattered upon the powdery sand. It feels a million miles away from Miami's bustle, with the occasional sound of laughing gulls soaring over weathered walkways on the dunes.

From Panama City west to Pensacola is Florida's Emerald Coast, named after the Gulf waters' color here. There are enough shimmering white sand beaches to satisfy anyone. Gulf Islands National Seashore stretches 150 miles west to Gulfport, Mississippi, its Santa Rosa Island section offering beaches, lagoons, wildlife, and historic Fort Pickens in its self-named state park.

As many marvels as the long coastline holds, Florida's interior is a trove of intriguing state parks, preserves, and historic sites. I was in awe walking the wooden boardwalk through old-growth cypress forest in the National Audubon Society's Corkscrew Swamp. At Devil's Millhopper State Geological Site, I climbed down the 120'-deep sink hole to discover lush ferns and plants more typical of the Appalachian Mountains than of Florida. Snorkeling is only one way to enjoy Ginnie Springs' crystal-clear waters, where turtles and fish gambol along the Santa Fe River. Canoeing the Loxahatchee River, a Wild and Scenic River, gave new meaning to the phrase "Real Florida." Driving through Ocala past thoroughbred horse farms with whitewashed fences bordered by roadside wildflowers further points up Florida's diversity.

Florida never disappoints in its colorful diversity. While many people at first think of Florida for its world-class theme parks and resorts, it is so much more: a water-and-land paradise so breath-taking that it will keep you coming back for more.

ABOVE: *Fishing and pleasure boats fill a Matecumbe Key marina.*

FACING PAGE: *Avian and human enjoy Indian Rocks Beach at Clearwater.*

ABOVE: *Windswept Pensacola Beach on the Gulf Coast.*

LEFT: *Once the winter retreat of International Harvester president James Deering, Vizcaya Museum and Gardens on Biscayne Bay exhibits European decorative arts in the 34-room mansion.*

Sea oats and fencing stabilize Santa Rosa Island's dunes along Gulf Island National Seashore.

ABOVE: *Bok Tower Gardens at Lake Wales holds 153 acres of plants and wildlife spreading around the carillon tower.*

FACING PAGE: *Ten Thousand Islands area in Everglades National Park.*

LEFT: *Water lily.*

BELOW: *Juvenile alligator.*

Snakebite Trail in Everglades National Park.

ABOVE: *Pelicans over Washington Oaks Beach.*

FACING PAGE: *West of Pensacola Beach, Fort Pickens State Park includes this coastal fortification dating from the Civil War.*

A hammock of sabal palms surrounded by cattails, along Tamiami Trail Scenic Highway through the Everglades.

Sunset over Naples Pier in the Gulf of Mexico.

Enjoying the evening along Ocean Drive amid Miami Beach's art deco architecture.

RENTAL
OCEAN KAYAK
OCEAN KAYAK
OCEAN KAYAK

ABOVE: *Bluestriped grunts at Molasses Reef in the Keys.*

RIGHT: *Manatees, placid mammals once called sea cows, are an endangered species.*

FACING PAGE: *Sailors on Boca Raton Beach.*

Fort Jefferson on Garden Key in Dry Tortugas National Park was built beginning in 1846, occupied by Union troops during the Civil War, used as an army prison until 1874 and as a naval wireless station into the early 1900s, and finally served as a World War I seaplane base.

ABOVE: *Sea grape leaves.*

FACING PAGE: *Stormy sunrise at Panama City.*

Fort Lauderdale Beach and Pier.

LEFT: *Ybor City, a National Historic Landmark District in Tampa, is filled with Spanish architectural detailing.*

BELOW: *Along South Beach at Miami Beach, a sand city arises.*

ABOVE: *Key West Lighthouse, dating from 1847, is open for tours.*

FACING PAGE: *Alexander Springs Recreation Area's namesake water.*

ABOVE: *Soft colors along the Suwannee River.*

FACING PAGE: *Cayo Costa State Park on the Gulf Coast.*

LEFT: *Night falls over the Gulf at Punta Gorda.*

BELOW: *Morning glory and shells, St. George Island State Park.*

RIGHT: *The Key West Aquarium.*

BELOW: *Mexico Beach on the Gulf Coast.*

In Ocala National Forest, Juniper Springs' output is 20 million gallons of water daily.

ABOVE: *Dock area at Vizcaya Museum and Gardens on Biscayne Bay.*

FACING PAGE: *Blowing Rocks Preserve, a project of The Nature Conservancy.*

St. Marks National Wildlife Refuge, along Apalachee Bay, covers 90,000 acres.

ABOVE: *Ca' d'Zan, at Sarasota, built in the 1920s for circus man John Ringling, is open for tours.*

FACING PAGE: *Alum Bluff rises 180 feet above the Apalachicola River near Bristol.*

ABOVE: *This replica lighthouse is part of a resort at Marathon on Key Vaca.*

FACING PAGE: *Naples Beach on Florida's west coast.*

RIGHT: *In 1832, John James Audubon was a guest in this Key West house while painting Florida wildlife.*

BELOW: *A space shuttle on exhibit at Kennedy Space Center, east of Orlando.*

FACING PAGE: *Water hyacinths along the Suwannee River, Manatee Springs State Park.*

ABOVE: *Ochopee, in south Florida, claims the United States' smallest post office.*

LEFT: *Phlox growing wild near Ocala.*

Fisher Island and the southern part of Miami Beach.

A sunset cruise at Key West.

Bromeliads grow on, but are not parasites to, cypress in Big Cypress National Preserve.

ABOVE: *Magnolias long have been a symbol of the Deep South.*

FACING PAGE: *In Highlands Hammock State Park.*

Shorebirds at Washington Oaks Gardens State Park.

ABOVE: *Ready to surf at Naples.*

FACING PAGE: *Long Key.*

14311
625

After the storm at Gulf Islands National Seashore.

ABOVE: *Blue Spring in Blue Spring State Park.*

FACING PAGE: *Bahia Honda State Park.*

ABOVE: *Sunset over Lake Hamilton.*

FACING PAGE: *Santa Rosa Island beach walkway and Gulf Shore dunes.*

ABOVE: *Sponge fishing boats.*

LEFT: *Cedar Key's tidal flats.*

LEFT: *"Swampy," a 200'-long alligator, advertises a reptile attraction at Christmas, east of Orlando.*

BELOW: *Mangroves flourish in areas like J.N. "Ding" Darling National Wildlife Refuge, which is flooded by ocean tides.*

FACING PAGE: *Lake Istakpoga cypress tree dressed in Spanish moss.*

The Bridge of Lions crosses the Matanzas River at St. Augustine.

A quiet lagoon at Long Key.

LEFT: *Seagulls scatter in flight.*

BELOW: *Pompano Beach.*

ABOVE: *Built between 1672 and 1695 of soft shell-rock, Castillo de San Marcos National Monument protected what was then Spain's northernmost colony in the Americas.*

RIGHT: *Belleair Beach on Sand Key near Clearwater.*

Corkscrew Swamp Sanctuary's cypress forest.

Ogden Pond in O'Leno State Park.

Springtime displays of redbud and Japanese magnolia at Alfred B. Maclay State Gardens, near Tallahassee.

The lighthouse at St. Marks National Wildlife Refuge overlooks Apalachee Bay.

Migrating waterfowl utilize the 19,000 acres of freshwater marsh and uplands in east-central Florida's Lake Woodruff National Wildlife Refuge.

LEFT: *Making it official.*

BELOW: *Pelicans on The Pier, St. Petersburg.*

New Smyrna Beach on the Atlantic Ocean.

ABOVE: *Myakka River State Park.*

FACING PAGE: *Seaside, a planned community east of Pensacola.*

ABOVE: *Anastasia State Recreation Area, St. Augustine Beach.*

RIGHT: *Oaks succumb to coastal erosion at Big Talbot Island State Park.*

Loxahatchee River marina at Jupiter Island, which boasts a red lighthouse.

SEASPORT

ABOVE: *A great blue heron in the Everglades.*

LEFT: *South Miami Beach shoreline access.*

The classic Don CeSar Beach Resort & Spa at St. Petersburg.

Early morning light paints a bewitching mood at Flamingo Bay.

ABOVE: *Ernest Hemingway's Key West home for most of the 1930s.*

FACING PAGE: *Eelgrass along Ginnie Springs Run, near High Springs.*

ABOVE: *A family moment on Naples Pier.*

FACING PAGE: *The Atlantic Ocean off Fort Lauderdale.*

RIGHT: *The Civil War battle of Olustee was Florida's largest, where a Confederate victory on February 20, 1864, sent Union troops retreating to Jacksonville.*

BELOW: *The Florida State Capitol in Tallahassee.*

Entering the 303 acres of Alfred B. Maclay State Gardens.

ABOVE: *Phlox field in Ocala National Forest.*

LEFT: *Lake Okeechobee's greatest depth is only twenty-four feet.*

Reflection pond at Cypress Gardens, Winter Haven.

LEFT: *A snowy egret.*

BELOW: *Cypress trees flourish along the river in Suwannee River State Park.*

ABOVE: *Edging the Gulf of Mexico, Bowman's Beach on Sanibel Island.*

RIGHT: *The shell-covered beach of Washington Oaks Gardens State Park.*

ABOVE: *Looking from Bahia Honda Key State Park to the causeway that connects the Keys to the mainland.*

LEFT: *The Florida Keys provide rich habitat for wildlife.*

Cypress trees border Lake Bradford.

ABOVE: *Historic architecture of South Beach along Miami Beach's Ocean Drive.*

LEFT: *The shifting sands of Gulf Islands National Seashore.*

ABOVE: *Fort Lauderdale's serpentine beach walkway.*

FACING PAGE: *Enjoying the Gulf Coast along Fort Walton Beach.*

The Loxahatchee, one of Florida's two Wild and Scenic Rivers, is lined with cypress and other trees.

ABOVE: *Scattered shells in Anastasia State Park.*

RIGHT: *Cormorants welcome a new day at Flamingo Bay, Everglades National Park.*

ABOVE: *South Beach lifeguard station at Miami Beach.*

FACING PAGE: *The Daytona Beach promenade is near the fishing pier and many amusements.*

FOLLOWING PAGE: *Dawn at Big Cypress National Preserve, the 2,400-square-mile south Florida home of endangered Florida panthers and other wildlife.*